DISCARD

HIP-HOP & R&B

Culture, Music & Storytelling

Bruno Mars

HIP-HOP & R&B

Culture, Music & Storytelling

MASON CREST

Chris Snellgrove

HIP-HOP & R&B
Bruno Mars

Culture, Music & Storytelling

Mason Crest
450 Parkway Drive, Suite D
Broomall, Pennsylvania 19008
(866) MCP-BOOK (toll free)

First printing
9 8 7 6 5 4 3 2 1

hardback: 978-1-4222-4178-3
series: 978-978-1-4222-4176-9
ebook: 978-1-4222-7620-4

Library of Congress Cataloging-in-Publication Data

Names: Snellgrove, Chris, author.
Title: Bruno Mars / Chris Snellgrove.
Description: Broomall, PA : Mason Crest, 2018. | Series: Hip-hop & R&B: culture, music & storytelling.
Identifiers: LCCN 2018020766 (print) | LCCN 2018022427 (ebook) | ISBN 9781422276204 (eBook) | ISBN 9781422241783 (hardback) | ISBN 9781422241769 (series)
Subjects: LCSH: Mars, Bruno, 1985---Juvenile literature. | Musicians--United States--Biography--Juvenile literature.
Classification: LCC ML3930.M318 (ebook) | LCC ML3930.M318 S64 2018 (print) | DDC 782.42164092 [B] --dc23
LC record available at https://lccn.loc.gov/2018020766

Developed and Produced by National Highlights, Inc.
Editor: Susan Uttendorfsky
Interior and cover design: Annalisa Gumbrecht, Studio Gumbrecht
Production: Michelle Luke

QR CODES AND LINKS TO THIRD-PARTY CONTENT

CONTENTS

KEY ICONS TO LOOK FOR:

Words to understand: These words with their easy-to-understand definitions will increase the reader's understanding of the text while building vocabulary skills.

Sidebars: This boxed material within the main text allows readers to build knowledge, gain insights, explore possibilities, and broaden their perspectives by weaving together additional information to provide realistic and holistic perspectives.

Educational videos: Readers can view videos by scanning our QR codes, providing them with additional educational content to supplement the text. Examples include news coverage, moments in history, speeches, iconic sports moments, and much more!

Text-dependent questions: These questions send the reader back to the text for more careful attention to the evidence presented there.

Research projects: Readers are pointed toward areas of further inquiry connected to each chapter. Suggestions are provided for projects that encourage deeper research and analysis.

Series of glossary of key terms: This back-of-the-book glossary contains terminology used throughout this series. Words found here increase the reader's ability to read and comprehend higher-level books and articles in this field.

Chapter 1

The Greatest Moments for Bruno Mars

Without a doubt, Bruno Mars has become a household name. He has sold millions of albums, has toured around the world, and has done the impossible as an artist: putting out new experimental albums that, simultaneously, are still able to deliver the same quality of his first hit album. For those trying to keep track of Mars and his achievements, it's easy to get dizzy amid the whirlwind of everything he has accomplished.

Fortunately, you don't need to become a pop culture historian to keep track Mars's career highlights. This will serve as a quick guide to the songs, albums, and tours that have taught us more about one of this generation's most defining musicians.

Billboard Breakout Success

Initially, Mars wanted to challenge himself. In a 2010 interview with *Rap-Up* magazine, he described feeling like he could "do more" than simply sing "cover songs" to "tourists." For a while, Mars had to be content with writing songs for others. However, when he stepped out of the

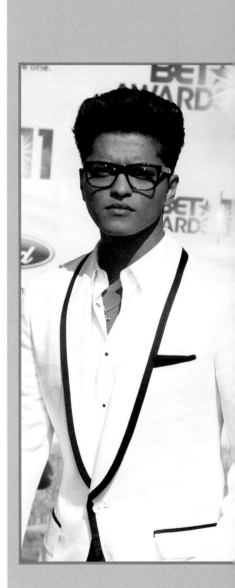

shadow of creating hit songs for other people and started writing successful songs for himself, the world took notice almost right away.

When he released the song *Just the Way You Are* in 2010, it shot all the way to the top of the *Billboard* Hot 100 Chart and put his first album, Doo-Wops and Hooligans, in the spotlight. This production was close to Mars's heart: In a 2010 interview with Idolator, he mentioned that "doo-wop" was what he called girls (specifically, his girlfriend) and "hooligans" was his nickname for boys. When he released the second single on this album, *Grenade*, on September 28, 2010, it also reached the top spot on the *Billboard* Hot 100. His third single, *The Lazy Song*, released on February 15, 2011, made it to number four on the *Billboard* Hot 100. The hit status and popularity of these songs resulted in strong sales of his first album—over 2.6 million in America and over 6 million worldwide.

Scan to watch the music video for *The Lazy Song*

Albums and World Tours

Doo-Wops and Hooligans rose to number three on the *Billboard* 200 after its release, eventually selling over 6 million copies by 2015 to fans in every corner of the world. The success of his music has brought many fans to his concerts, and the Doo-Wops and Hooligans Tour ran for

Bruno Mars
HIP-HOP & R&B

two years (from November 16, 2010, to January 28, 2012) to promote that first album. The tour also marked a major transition for Mars, as he had previously been the opening act for bands such as Maroon 5 (in the later part of their Hands All Over Tour, starting in October 6, 2010), or had to share the spotlight with other artists, such as Travie McCoy on his tour through Europe that started October 18, 2010.

Now, with breakout singles and a hit album, Mars solidified himself as a leading man and the music industry recognized it. He went on later successful tours, including one promoting his second album, Unorthodox Jukebox (that Moonshine Jungle Tour lasted from June 22, 2013, to October 18, 2014), and a tour called the 24K Magic World Tour to promote his third album. It began on March 28, 2017, and, as of this writing, is still ongoing. Each of his three major tours has been worldwide.

Watch the official music video for *Grenade*

Remembering His Roots

While Mars stopped being the opening act for others, he has continued collaborating with other musicians (including Wiz Khalifa, Snoop Dogg, and Mark Ronson) as a way of building his brand and furthering his fan base. More on that later!

Awards Veteran

While some artists may take time to get the professional respect they deserve, Mars established himself very early, with his first album landing him a whopping six Grammy Awards nominations. While that would have been impressive enough, he won the Grammy Award for Best Male Vocal Performance for his song *Just the Way You Are* in 2011.

He continued to receive nominations in subsequent years, and ended up winning several more times. In 2014, the Grammy Award for Best Pop Vocal Album became his for Unorthodox Jukebox, and in 2016, the Grammy Award for Record of the Year was presented to Uptown Funk. That same year, he also won the Grammy Award for Album of the Year as producer for The Smeezingtons' album 25. The production team Mars created, The Smeezingtons, also includes Philip Lawrence and Ari Levine.

Truly Impressive

Mars's songs stand on their own as major achievements, but the sheer number of nominations and awards he's received is extraordinarily rare for such a young music artist. The level of success he has gained for a singer in his early thirties caused an uproar in some

Bruno Mars —
It Will Rain
(Doo Wops
& Hooligans
Tour Live)

corners of the music industry. At the 2013 MTV VMAs (Video Music Awards), Kanye West claimed that Mars's feats were a product of music industry manipulation designed to get people to vote for the "prettiest" musician.

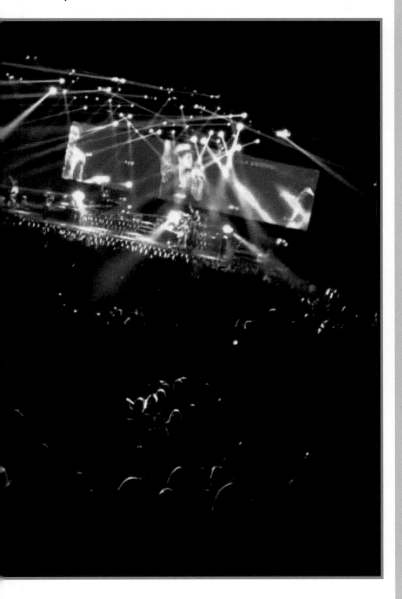

Scan to watch the the music video for *Unorthodox Jukebox*

Scan here
to listen to
Young, Wild & Free

Scan to watch
Bubble Butt
with over
62,007,332 views

Collaborations

- *Billionaire*, featuring Travie McCoy (2010)

- *Nothin' on You*, featuring B.o.B. (2010)

- *Young, Wild & Free*, featuring Snoop Dogg and Wiz Khalifa (2011)

- *Mirror*, featuring Lil Wayne (2011)

- *Lighters*, featuring Bad Meets Evil (2011)

- *Walls Come Down*, featuring Keke Palmer (2011)

- *6 AM (Remix)*, featuring Bueno (2012)

- *Can't Come Back to Me*, featuring Layzie Boy (2012)

- *Bubble Butt*, featuring Major Lazer (2013)

- *Uptown Funk*, featuring Mark Ronson (2015)

Greatest Yet to Come?

We have seen a number of truly great moments with Mars—his hit songs, his colorful collaborations, and his string of awards. However, since each new album has been more impressive than the one that came before, it's entirely possible that the greatest moments for Bruno Mars haven't even happened yet. Fittingly, he is

Snoop Dog collaborated with Bruno Mars on Young, Wild & Free

a man often trying to outdo his own legacy: An old *New York Times* piece described him as a man trying to escape "a shadow of his own making" due to his previous achievements. That blurb was published when his first album had just debuted. Considering his runaway success since then, that shadow has only grown.

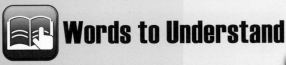
percussionist: someone who plays a percussion instrument, such as the drums, the triangle, or the tambourine.

performative: this adjective refers to anything relating to the idea of an artist's performance.

shoehorned: to force someone or something into a space it is not suited for it, usually against that person or thing's will.

homage: to pay special honor or attention to someone or something.

Chapter 2

Never Alone on the Road to the Top

Mars's Family Life
Parents

Some of the most influential people in Mars's life were his parents. To put it mildly, they were very musical: His dad, Pete Hernandez, is a **percussionist** who specialized in playing Latin music, while his mother, Bernadette San Pedro Hernandez (née Bayot) was a hula dancer and singer who died in 2013. When Bruno Mars was born on October 8, 1985, his parents were performing a show together in Hawaii. Through their mutual love of music, they encouraged Mars's musical and **performative** talents from the age of two, giving him the confidence to step out on his own as a musician.

Siblings

Mars has several siblings, and all of them have played a major part in his life. For instance, his older brother Eric has held the drummer spot for years in Mars's band, The Hooligans. His four sisters (Presley Hernandez, Tiara Hernandez, Jaime Kailani, and Tahiti Hernandez) are very musical as well, being part of an all-girl singing group known as The Lylas.

Jaime is arguably the sibling that Mars is closest to because he lived with her when he first moved to Los Angeles. More on that soon! Also, Mars has played a major role in supporting the charity that Jaime started called Mama Earth.

The Family Business

The Love Notes

Mars's parents didn't stop singing and grooving when he was born. Instead, they created a family band called The Love Notes, in which they were all performers for various venues on Waikiki Beach in Hawaii. As performers, they did a good job of maintaining variety, playing music that ranged from classic Motown funk to the kind of doo-wop music Mars named his first album after.

In between the music, they offered crowds impressions of famous celebrities to maximize the entertainment value. Mars joined the band when he was four and performed in it until he was eleven, when it broke up due to the divorce of his parents. This time period was very important to Mars's development as a musician. He recalls having ready access to a variety of instruments that became crucial to increasing his musical skills.

It also built his legendary skill as a performer: From the age of four, Mars's specialty was impressions of Elvis Presley. He quickly stole the show, becoming known far and wide as "Little Elvis." To this day, fans enjoy watching a young Mars shuffle

Watch this video
to see a young
Bruno Mars as
"Little Elvis"

and sing as an Elvis impersonator via recordings on YouTube. It seems as though Mars knew he was destined for greater things than simply copying other musicians.

Later, Mars looked back on that time with amusement. In a 2014 interview with the *Star-Advertiser*, a local Hawaiian newspaper, he described his younger self as being "two feet tall, with the hair and the glittery gold suit," but he dismissed the silly appearance by declaring, "That's where I was back then."

Education

Mars had a relatively humble education, attending different public institutions in Hawaii like, for elementary school, Pearl City Elementary. Then he attended Robert Louis Stevenson Middle School. High school was an easy trip for the future star, as he went to President Theodore Roosevelt High School, which was very close to his middle school. During high school, the primary expression of Mars's musical talents came through a band called The School Boys that began in 2000.

After graduating in 2003, Mars decided to not pursue higher education. Instead, he moved to Los Angeles less than a year later, when he was only seventeen, so he could pursue his dream of becoming a music star.

Hints of the Future—While Mars's education was simple enough, he had a band while in high school. It was formed with three other boys, and they specialized in playing classic oldies. This experience helped to further cement his dreams of a professional music career.

First Major Album Debut

The road to the top was not easy for Mars, nor was it nearly as quick as he imagined it would be, and the rocky path included being dropped by Motown Records after being signed on and encountering racism in the industry. He demo'd *Nothin' on You* to an unnamed executive who loved it, but wanted to give the song to a white singer. He discovered a taste of early success by writing hit songs for other people, such as *Right Round* for Flo Rida, *One Day* for Matisyahu, *Lost* for Menudo, and so on. But the young man still yearned to sing his own hit songs and become a breakout star. In a 2010 *Entertainment Weekly* interview, he described becoming a music producer first as an act performed "out of frustration" that he couldn't sell his songs with himself as the artist.

That finally happened when he released Doo-Wops and Hooligans, an album that managed to be a kind of pure synthesis of the young man's life. Mars signed a contract with Atlantic Records in 2009, leading to his debut album's worldwide hit. Stylistically and musically, the recording played **homage** to the brand of doo-wop music that his father had brought from the continental United States to Hawaii.

As much as the album honored his father, though, it also presented Mars as an artist unlike any the world had seen before. Hit song after hit song burst out of the album, including *Grenade, Just the Way You Are*, and *The Lazy Song*. This first production showed his range as a singer and highlighted his ability to create catchy songs without being **shoehorned** into a single genre, such as "love songs." He learned to channel his feelings into this album, including his own pain. In a Just Jared interview in 2010, he described *Grenade* as a song in which the listener heard Mars "suffer," and said that he truly wanted "to bring the emotion to life."

Team Effort

Considering how explosive his popularity has been, many people are shocked to discover how few albums Mars has created (as of this writing, only three major works). After all, it seems as if he has been responsible for so much more music than that. And in a way, he has been: More than almost any other artist, Mars seems to understand the importance of teaming up with other singers and songwriters and using the collaborations as opportunities to further build his brand. He has performed alongside artists that fans might never associate with Mars himself, including Wiz Khalifa, Snoop Dogg, and Lil Wayne. These artists are noted for songs about extreme drug use and violence, which are very different from Mars's gentle vibe, but the singer's purpose is clear: to use these collaborations as introductions to fans of other musicians and genres who are unlikely to check out a Bruno Mars album on their own.

Here is a breakdown of some of Mars's most famous connections on his way to the top:

Nothin' on You, featuring B.o.B.
(Released December 15, 2009)

Just as Mars helped Travie McCoy launch his solo career, he helped rapper B.o.B. kick off the single from

Wiz Khalifa arrives at the Wango Tango Concert at The Home Depot Center on May 12, 2012, in Carson, CA

his debut album. *Nothin' on You* was written in part by Mars, and his vocals were also featured in the song, which came out in 2009. While Mars did not tour with B.o.B., it was at that time that he founded The Smeezingtons, the production team that generated the album.

The song itself is something of a hybrid, combining pop and hip-hop elements with a Southern twang. The hybrid nature can also be seen in the very different styles of Mars and B.o.B., with Mars offering a sweet, crooning melody while B.o.B. spits rapid-fire rap lyrics that are as inventive as they are fast. Lyrically, the track serves as a very unconventional love song in which the singer points out how he sees beautiful girls everywhere he travels, but they have "nothin' on" the girl whom he truly loves.

Travie McCoy at Cartoon Network's first ever Hall of Game Awards, Barker Hanger, Santa Monica, CA.

Billionaire, featuring Travie McCoy
(Released March 09, 2010)

One of the catchiest collaborations that Mars recorded was *Billionaire*. The song came about through a partnership with Travie McCoy that included writing and touring. Mars had written and produced songs for him previously, and then they toured Europe together in October and November of 2010. McCoy has a background in both punk rock and rap rock, and he previously dazzled the world with his band, Gym Class Heroes, before striking out on his own. His first solo album, Lazarus, featured *Billionaire* as its lead single, and Mars helped the song shine.

The song itself is a mixture of reggae and soft rock, and the whimsical lyrics about a poor singer's earnest desire to be rich offer moments of poignancy, too. Some of the lines are about using the money to take care of the singer's friends and family rather than being completely selfish with it.

Young, Wild & Free, featuring Snoop Dogg and Wiz Khalifa
(Released October 11, 2011)

This is perhaps the most laid-back collaboration Mars has recorded so far. Mars had not previously toured with the two singers, but he sang in their song *Young, Wild & Free*, assisting with the creation of the catchy hook, and even helping to produce it.

While Snoop Dogg and Wiz Khalifa—two veteran rap and hip-hop singers with a tendency to incorporate lyrics about drugs and partying—may seem very different from Mars's style, the song actually evokes nostalgia for an idyllic past. This sentimental love for the past is something Mars has been taking advantage of since he first made waves as the world's youngest Elvis impersonator. With his smooth hook, listeners of all ages can feel as if they too are "young and wild and free."

Lil Wayne performs at Sleep Train Amphitheater on September 03, 2011, in Wheatland, CA

Mirror, featuring Lil Wayne
(Released September 13, 2011)

The best part of any music collaboration is when two creators construct something unique. That was the case when it came to the song *Mirror*, which Mars worked on with Lil Wayne. The song, released in 2011, represents their only partnership so far, as Mars has not appeared on any more songs with Lil Wayne and has not toured with him.

Lil Wayne is primarily known for his very irreverent brand

of hip-hop. This song portrays the singer looking into a mirror and ruminating about everything from his parents to his past, all while struggling to determine how he should change in the future. As for Mars, he contributes a fairy tale dialogue into the track, personifying Lil Wayne's burning questions about why he keeps returning to reflect on his life if the world is truly supposed to accept him as he is.

In their mutual understanding of what it is like to struggle with acceptance, fame, and living in a father's shadow, these two megastars truly bonded throughout this joint effort.

Lighters, featuring Bad Meets Evil
(Released June 14, 2011)

With musical collaborations, it's sometimes very clear when one artist has rubbed off on the other. This is the case with the single *Lighters*, which Mars worked on with the group Bad Meets Evil. The song came out in 2011 and was co-written by Mars, but he never toured with the group.

Bad Meets Evil is primarily known for a certain brand of hip-hop music since the group is composed of Eminem and Royce da 5'9". But this song, co-written by Mars and featuring his voice, has a variety of soul, alternative rock, and even synthetic pop styles. This is clearly Mars's influence—he loves mixing up multiple varieties. The song includes a lot of bravado about the singers' rise to music superstar status, though Mars anchors the theme with lyrics about the power of discovering and living out one's dreams. Even alongside a legendary rapper like Eminem, Mars shines as a genuine inspiration.

Bubble Butt, featuring Major Lazer
(Released May 24, 2013)

It's clear from any interview that Mars is a man with deep feelings and sensitivity. Beneath the pop star exterior—with legions of fans and awards—is someone thoughtful and introspective. Of course, he has a wild side, too, and that is on display in his collaboration with Major Lazer on the song *Bubble Butt*. The song came out in 2013, and while Mars never toured with Major Lazer, he co-wrote the lyrics.

Eminem

The track focuses on a mischievous description of the singer's love life while Mars sings the hook—comprised almost entirely of singing "bubble butt" over and over again. The song alternates between being raunchy and silly, and the bona fide electronic dance music hit brought Mars and his sound into clubs.

Mark Ronson

Uptown Funk, featuring Mark Ronson
(Released November 10, 2014)

Hands down, the greatest musical partnership Mars has experienced so far was the song *Uptown Funk* with Mark Ronson, which came out in 2014. The two never toured together, but this song was so influential to Mars's career that they performed it alongside Beyoncé at the fiftieth Super Bowl in California in 2016. While Mars was undeniably a gifted musician and exuberant artist, Beyoncé is a worldwide brand unto herself, and they managed to collectively dazzle fans in one of the most important moments in the ongoing success of his brand.

This was good news for Mars because of the effort he put into the song. He and Ronson spent months recording and perfecting the track, and subsequently, it spent months at the top of the charts. For as much work as the two expended in polishing everything, the song itself comes off as pure breezy fun, with silly lyrics about looking beautiful and attracting admiring women.

However, the single is so good and popular that it became a double-edged sword for Mars. He claimed that one of the reasons for the delay between his second and third albums was that it was difficult for him to follow up after the most successful song he ever created!

Never-Ending Road

It's easy for fans to look at the success Mars has experienced, with both his solo music and hit collaborations, and assume that the artist has safely made it to the top. Interestingly, though, Mars himself disagrees with such notions. When accepting the Innovator Award from iHeartRadio, he said,

> It's a little ironic for me because I genuinely feel like I'm just getting started. So, buckle up. I don't know where we're going yet, but we're going— keep up!

He treats each new album and each new collaboration as a chance to challenge himself as a musician and as an artist. Going by what Mars said, it seems he has no intentions of resting on his previous successes. Instead, he'll keep producing better and better music for the world to enjoy. And while the singer's personal journey as an artist and musician may never be finished, the rest of us are able to happily enjoy the ride.

Text-Dependent Questions:

❶ Whom did Mars sing with on the song *Mirror*?

❷ What was the name of the high school that Mars attended?

❸ What was Mars's most successful collaboration?

Research Project:

Listen to three (or more) of the collaborations that Mars has created with others. Write about which one of them you consider the best. Pay special attention to what you think Mars himself contributed to the song, and how and why he helped make it successful.

diversity:
the inclusion of individuals representing more than one national origin, color, religion, socioeconomic level, sexual orientation, etc.

reggae:
a style of music that originated in Jamaica and was popularized by music artists such as Bob Marley.

minimalist:
someone who believes in the idea of minimalism, which is the use of simple forms to create a reaction in a viewer or listener.

Chapter 3

Hip-Hop Statistics Highlight Mars's Success

From Unknown to Unstoppable

Bruno Mars has enjoyed the kind of career that mirrors his own passionate nature. While he started from very humble beginnings and struggled to be taken seriously (including an aforementioned deal with Motown Records that fell through, and struggles with racism within the music industry), he eventually signed a contract for his debut album. It absolutely exploded, making him a household name. Mars has been rightfully honored with a number of awards over the years, and it is also very easy to track his continuing success by monitoring the sales of his three albums.

Sales

Doo-Waps and Hooligans
(Released October 04, 2010)

Mars's first album cemented him as a musician to be reckoned with when not one but two *Billboard* Hot 100 number one tracks burst off it: *Just the Way You Are* and *Grenade*. He intended the album to be a tribute to the doo-wop music that his father brought to the islands of Hawaii, which Mars grew up learning to play as part of his family's band.

He imagined he would be reinventing himself when he left Hawaii and moved to Los Angeles, and that part came true when this album received five Grammy Award nominations for the 54th Grammys, including Album of the Year. But it was solidly fixed in his roots, and the RIAA certified Doo-Wops and Hooligans five-times Platinum in June 2016, which means over five million copies have been sold or streamed since its release in 2010. The success proves that the world likes the young singer just as he is.

Unorthodox Jukebox
(Released December 07, 2012)

Mars released his follow-up album, Unorthodox Jukebox, two years later. This production did an excellent job of highlighting the **diversity** of skills that Mars has as a performer. Instead of focusing on the successful doo-wop style of the first album, Mars experimented with many different styles. The album had tracks from rock to **reggae** to disco to soul, and listening to it was like walking alongside Mars through a history of music. Fortunately, his fans were very happy to see him stretching his skills, and this album has also sold over 6 million copies.

The release became the fastest selling solo artist album of 2012, and was eventually certified as triple Platinum by the RIAA. It was a hit online and offline, too, with that Platinum certification coming from millions of albums moved through both traditional sales and digital streaming. Overall, the recording proved that Mars could still leverage artistic experimentation into worldwide acclaim, critical success, and passionate fan devotion.

24K MAGIC
(Released November 18, 2016)

Mars's third album, 24K MAGIC, was released in 2016 and showed up on the *Billboard* 200 Chart at number two. As with the production before it, its debut highlighted his continuing success, as all his releases have debuted within the top three on the *Billboard* 200 Chart. The style showcased the need Mars has for stretching his own artistic boundaries. Toward this end, it kept the funk and soul elements that were popular in UNORTHODOX JUKEBOX while adding

elements and the influence of 1990s R&B acts such as Boyz II Men. As an experiment in R&B, it was wildly successful.

Not only did Mars successfully land at the apex of the Top R&B/Hip-Hop Album *Billboard* Charts in the first month of the album's release, but the recording has not come off the R&B Album Chart as of September 2017. The album was certified double Platinum within a year, with almost 2 million sales, and it appears to be another worldwide megahit for Mars.

Sweeping the 2018 Grammy Awards

Held in Madison Square Garden, in New York City, Bruno Mars swept the night's most coveted awards. His funk-infused album 24K MAJIC, won Album of the Year, and the song *That's What I Like*, won song of the year. Mars won in four other categories: Best R&B Performance, Best R&B Album, Best R&B Song and Best Engineered Album, Non-Classical. By night's end Mars was the year's most decorated artist.

Endorsements
Bench (2011)

There's no two ways around it: Bruno Mars is a handsome man. It's not very surprising, then, that he loaned both his good looks and his star power to a clothing company. In 2011, Mars provided endorsements for the British clothing company Bench. The two simplistic ads helped channel a **minimalist** hipster cool, and as an endorsement, this is very "on brand" for Mars. These advertisements helped establish him as a young, rebellious artist who has both style and poise.

Chromatik (2012)

Click here to watch a Bench commercial with Bruno Mars

Sometimes it makes perfect sense when a celebrity endorses a particular product, and this is exactly what happened with Mars and Chromatik. This company created an app to help consumers learn how to write and play, as well as produce, their own music. Considering that Mars began his career producing music created by other people, his teaming up with Chromatik to help bring others' music dreams to life was a great fit. Not only did he endorse the company, but he invested in it and continues to promote the app by including his music on it.

Getting the endorsement of someone like Mars was also a major coup for Chromatik. By joining forces with a worldwide megastar, Chromatik is attempting to situate itself as a premiere app for would-be musicians.

Njoy (2013)

At first, many people were shocked to see that Mars invested in Njoy. Why would he endorse electronic cigarettes?

It turns out that Mars made a promise to his mother to quit smoking, and he decided to keep that promise after she passed away in 2013. To this end, he uses electronic cigarettes to try to kick the habit, and the star invested in the company to assist other smokers to become tobacco-free. It's easy to see how attractive this product is to Mars himself, as he has a pretty well-known habit of intense smoking, especially when he is working on a new album. Rolling Stone mentioned witnessing Mars smoking "his umpteenth cigarette of the day" during an interview when the singer was finishing work on 24K MAGIC.

Tight Lips—Mars has not spoken publicly much about his mother's death and how it affected him. Making this endorsement was actually one of the strongest early statements he made concerning it. He didn't really open up about how her 2013 death affected him until a 2017 interview with *People* magazine.

Pepsi (2014)

One of Mars's music idols while growing up was Michael Jackson, and after "Little Elvis" got a little older, he added Michael Jackson to the list of famous celebrities he imitated as part of the family business back in Hawaii. After he became a megastar, he was able to emulate Jackson in a different way by scoring an endorsement deal from Pepsi. While this product is a bit more straightforward than others that Mars endorses, it shows his staying power as a worldwide artist who is his own name brand.

SelvaRey Rum (2015)

Not content simply to have endorsement deals with other beverages, Mars co-founded SelvaRey Rum, which specializes in producing Panama-style rums. These distilled spirits have won multiple awards throughout the years, and in 2015, their distribution stretched from the West Coast to the East Coast, and even to Hawaii. A successful, nationally distributed line of rum highlights Mars's willingness to take a more entrepreneurial role in the influential and famous world that he is now a major part of by creating his own products rather than simply endorsing others.

Awards

The number of awards he has won highlights the universal appeal of Mars and his songs.

American Music Awards
Favorite Pop/Rock Male Artist | Won in 2011

American Society of Composers, Authors, and Publishers
Most Performed Songs—*Billionaire, Nothin' on You,* and *Just the Way You Are* | Won in 2011

Song of the Year—*Just The Way You Are* | Won in 2011

Most Performed Songs—*Grenade, The Lazy Song,* and *Lighters* | Won in 2012

Most Performed Songs—*It Will Rain and Young, Wild & Free* | Won in 2013

Most Performed Songs—*Locked out of Heaven, When I Was Your Man,* and *Treasure* | Won in 2014

Most Performed Songs—*Uptown Funk* | Won in 2016

Most Performed Songs—*24K Magic* and *Uptown Funk* | Won in 2017

ASCAP's Rhythm & Soul Music Awards
Top Rap Song—*Nothin' on You* | Won in 2011

Award Winning R&B/Hip-Hop and Rap Songs—*Uptown Funk* | Won in 2016

APRA Music Awards
International Work of the Year—*Uptown Funk* | Won in 2016

BET Awards
Best Male R&B/Pop Artist | Won in 2017

Video of the Year—*24K Magic* | Won in 2017

Billboard Latin Music Awards
Crossover Artist of the Year | Won in 2014

Billboard Music Awards
Top Radio Song—*Just the Way You Are* | Won in 2011

Grammy Awards
Best Male Pop Vocal Performance—*Just the Way You Are* | Won in 2011

Best Pop Vocal Album—Unorthodox Jukebox | Won in 2014

Record of the Year—Uptown Funk | Won in 2016

Best Pop Duo/Group Performance—*Uptown Funk* | Won in 2016 with Mark Ronson

Record of the Year – 24K Magic / Won in 2018

Song of the Year – *That's What I Like* / Won in 2018

MTV Video Music Awards
Best Male Video—*Locked out of Heaven* | Won in 2013

Best Choreography—*Treasure* | Won in 2013

People's Choice Awards
Favorite Male Artist | Won in 2012

Teen Choice Awards
Choice Music: Breakout Artist | Won in 2011

Choice Summer: Music Star—Male | Won in 2011

Choice Music: R&B Artist | Won in 2013

Choice Music Star—Male | Won in 2013

Hollywood Walk of Fame
Bruno Mars was added to the Hollywood Walk of Fame's
2016 roster in the category of "recording."

The Triple Threat

Overall, Mars is a force to be reckoned with on three different fronts. He has the continuous success in album sales and digital downloads that most artists only dream of. He has major endorsements for a variety of different products, ensuring that the average consumer is likely to run into Mars wherever they go. Finally, he has a string of awards that highlights his growing importance to both the music industry and to the world.

No one but Mars knows what the singer will do next. But based on everything we've seen so far, it's sure to be nothing less than epic. And this already-impressive list of awards is only going to grow as time goes on!

Text-Dependent Questions:

❶ What Grammy Award did Mars win in 2011?

❷ What Grammy Award did Mars win in 2014?

❸ What is the name of the product that Bruno Mars helped create in 2015?

Research Project:

Examine the different endorsements that Mars has made, and write about which one you think best represents the singer, and which one does the worst job of representing the singer. Pay special attention to how these endorsements affect how you view Mars, his image, and his reputation.

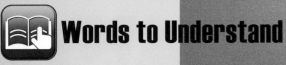 **Words to Understand**

innovator:
someone who offers a new idea or way of thinking.

swagger:
a noun, verb, or adjective used to describe the confident way that a person walks, talks, or otherwise acts.

collectively:
to do something as part of a group.

Chapter 4

Good Music, Meaningful Lyrics, and Hard Work Intersect

I f you want to discover who a musician really is, you need to pay attention to his or her messaging and branding. While the message and brand are not always completely accurate, discovering how artists wish to be seen by the world is a great way to find out what they value and who they want to be.

In the case of Mars, we can discover who he is by looking at key speeches and interviews, as well as some of his most famous lyrics.

Bruno Mars, Innovator

Mars has won a number of awards over the years, giving many acceptance speeches. One of his better ones came when he was presented with the **Innovator** Award at the iHeartRadio Music Awards on March 05, 2017, in Inglewood. The speech helped to highlight Mars's humility, as he took the time to thank his band and credit them as a creative muse.

We've come a long way… We used to play bars, 200-seater rooms, and now you've seen these guys in the videos, you've seen 'em at the Super Bowl. This is my family right here. … These are the guys that make me wanna be better and be great.

Of course, Mars honored his fans during the speech as well.

I want to thank the fans in the building and the fans at home. I love you guys. I do this all for you guys. You make me wanna be a better songwriter, a better performer, and a better entertainer.

Not wanting to let everything get too cheesy and emotional, though, Mars noted that it was "a little ironic" that he would get such a prestigious award…

…because I genuinely feel like I'm just getting started. So, buckle up. I don't know where we're going yet, but we're going—keep up!

From anyone else, this would sound like ego. From Mars, it is simply a promise.

Confidence and Swagger

While Mars definitely presents himself as more of a lover than a fighter, he would never be mistaken for a pushover "nice guy." Part of the reason is because he has worked hard to build his particular brand, wanting it to express a lot of confidence and **swagger**. This was demonstrated in an interview that Mars gave to UK-based *The Independent* in December 2012. He appeared unfazed by the idea that some people might not like his latest album. He told the interviewer, "I really feel so strong about it … If you don't like it, then there's nothing I can do; there's no way I can make it better." Then he laughed with the confidence of a man with several hit songs under his belt.

Mars's swagger comes from the fact that he is not content to rest on his previous achievements and proven hits. He constantly tries something bold and new. In that same interview, he said,

> *I want to sing about new things and I want to experiment with my music. I want to evolve lyrically and sonically and, production-wise, I wanna keep pushing myself to try new things. I never want to feel like I'm taking the safe route or the easy way.*

Considering how successful his various albums have been, it's safe to say that Mars has proven his talent time and time again as he continues to experiment, showing that his cocky swagger is well-earned!

Fast Fact 3:

Proving Himself—It's possible that Mars's need to constantly change his style is related to his father's shows. They varied in style and presentation so they would appeal to more people.

Known as a Perfectionist

Despite the huge appeal of his songs and albums, Mars is the first to admit that success comes at a cost. In an industry dominated by big personalities and bigger egos, Mars has not lost the perfectionist edge that drove him to create music in the first place. At times, that need for perfectionism has driven him to bad habits: In a *Rolling Stone* interview, he recalls chain-smoking day after day and virtually living inside a recording studio for eighteen months. Despite the intense pressure to complete 24K MAGIC and release it, Mars wanted to make sure each track was perfect, often revising them dozens of times. This led to *Rolling Stone* affectionately dubbing him "obsessive" and a "pop perfectionist."

Interestingly, the editing process Mars uses to perfect his work is very down-to-earth. He admits that he doesn't use complex musical theory to figure out why a song has trouble spots. Instead, he says, "I'm just trying to figure out why I'm tuning out in certain parts." It's a simple line, but a revealing one, displaying that Mars is simultaneously his biggest fan and his harshest critic. He's not willing to release anything to the public until it is good enough for him.

Smooth Operator to Bad Boy

It's not surprising that Mars started out with a relatively squeaky-clean reputation. After all, his performing experiences began with participation in his family's entertainment show, and the first time he had worldwide fame, it was as a cute impersonator of musicians such as Elvis Presley and Michael Jackson. However, the artist used his third major album, 24K MAGIC, to rebrand himself. Mars was well aware of his reputation of being sweet and lightweight as a singer. When asked about this in a 2012 CBS interview, Mars clarified that critics who felt this way could "go to hell."

Apparently, the album makeover worked: *Vice* magazine reported it was the album in which Mars went from being a "moist dishcloth" to a "swaggering" musician. They credited him with discovering how to use everything from impossibly catchy basslines to a willingness to pursue funky beats and crazy songs instead of focusing on the tired genre of romantic music. And while their description of early Mars as a "moist dishcloth" is more than a bit unfair, *Vice* seems to have a point—his third

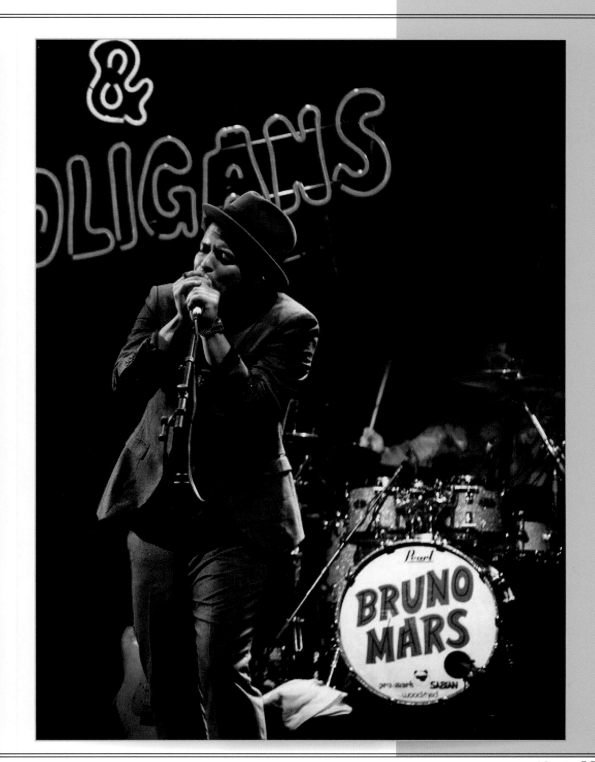

album secured a place for Mars within the world of hip-hop as easily as he previously secured his place in other genres.

Fast Fact 4:

Delicate Balance—Mars has been very selective in how he introduces himself to other genres of music, typically doing so through hit collaborations. This may be, in part, because of the early difficulty that recording companies had with deciding how to market him. He recalled one executive who wanted to use *Nothin' on You* to make "the next thing" out of a "white artist"—rather than Mars himself.

Watch Bruno Mars and Beyoncé performing at the Super Bowl

Famous Lyrics

Grenade

This song crafted Mars's reputation as a faithful, romantic partner. The lyrics juxtapose vivid images of violence and pain with the notion that the singer will go through these things for the sake of his love. On its own, this would have already been a powerful statement on the idea of love and self-sacrifice. However, Mars adds a twist, stating outright that he knows his love won't reciprocate.

Most people have been in lopsided relationships, so his

listeners can relate to this. Moreover, it showcases how this particular pain—of loving someone who cannot or will not return—hurts more than the violent acts described in such detail. Mars feels this way himself, telling NPR in a 2010 interview that "It's probably the worst feeling in the world, when you're deeply and madly in love with a woman and you know she's not feeling you the same way, and you don't know why."

Just the Way You Are

Mars is known for his beautiful lyrics, and this song spotlights his empathy. The down-to-earth words reveal that he understands his listeners' worries and fears and hopes the song can provide comfort. In *Just the Way You Are*, the singer expresses his conviction that the woman he loves should never feel the need to change. Mars seems to understand the pressure on women to alter how they look or act to please others. To them, he offers the assurance that the real key to perfection is the person inside. It's a powerful message, and with these lyrics, Mars sets the bar high for romantic partners everywhere!

The Lazy Song

Of course, not all of Mars's tracks are about relationships. Sometimes he channels something that all his fans can easily relate to. In *The Lazy Song*, he gives voice to an idea that there's nothing wrong with being lazy from time to time. And while the lyrics are obviously humorous, Mars still manages to embed a deeper meaning, effectively becoming an advocate on the idea of self-care. It is okay for people to hold the expectations and responsibilities of the world at bay to have some time to themselves. Considering the busy and crowded spheres that Mars lives and works in, this is definitely a sentiment that the star can understand, and one that most of his fans can appreciate.

When I Was Your Man

Balancing romance and melancholy is a familiar theme in Mars's songs. This one begins with the premise that Mars has broken up with someone who is now dating someone else. Rather than be angry, the theme highlights that Mars wishes nothing but good things for his ex-partner. While that is a positive message, the singer made it heartbreaking by including the fact that the singer realizes all the things he did wrong in the relationship. Now he understands exactly what he should have done, but he cannot change the past and must be content with wishing that someone else will be a better partner. Ultimately, this song blends haunting beauty and lasting regret into something unforgettable.

Final Thoughts

It can be pretty difficult to pin Mars down. Like his music, it seems the man constantly changes who and what he is. However, his words—whether in interviews, lyrics, or simple conversation— reveal a man of great depth and passion. He has been careful to build a brand in such a way that it doesn't compromise his core identity or values, and this makes him as rare as the 24K magic that he sings about!

It will be fascinating to see what future albums and collaborations Mars puts out. Will he continue to walk the fine line between giving his legions of fans the kind of sound and performance they want, while also challenging himself to create sounds he has never tried before? Ironically, the artist who sings about how people are perfect as they are has never been content with his own work, constantly seeking perfection through the evolution of his music.

Text-Dependent Questions:

❶ What is the singer's relationship to the woman in *When I Was Your Man*?

❷ The words in *Grenade* insist that he will catch a grenade for the woman he loves, but what surprising thing do we learn about her devotion to Mars?

❸ In what album did Mars attempt to portray more of a "bad boy" persona?

Research Project:

Examine at least three of Mars's songs that focus on his relationships with others. Write about which of the lyrics you think provide the most honest description of a modern relationship. Why are these particular lyrics so accurate? Why are the other lyrics less accurate?

Words to Understand

posh:
typically used as an adjective to describe something as being particularly fancy, stylish, and/or extravagant.

mutant:
someone or something that is unnatural because it has undergone a state of mutation; also, a derogatory term to mock someone for not fitting in with a particular group.

aneurysm:
a medical term describing extremely swollen arteries that are caused by deteriorating artery walls.

Chapter 5

Not Forgetting the Community Despite Personal Adversity

Foundations and Charities

Happily, Mars has not been satisfied to keep his good fortune to himself. He shares both his money and his talent by working with a number of different foundations. One of those foundations, fittingly enough, is affiliated with the Grammy Awards!

The GRAMMY Foundation

Previously, Mars worked with the GRAMMY Foundation to offer students financial aid for their college education through the Mars Scholarship Fund that he initiated in 2014. Owing to his bigheartedness, Mars is also attempting to make things easier for the next struggling student who is a lot like he was. The money for his scholarship fund was raised by the Hawaii Community Foundation, under Mars's guidance, and he requested that preference for the award be given to Hawaiian students. With his help, winners of this award will complete their own musical journey, and approximately 105 applicants are selected to attend the "Grammy Camp" each year.

Musicians On Call

One of the most touching organizations that Mars is involved with is Musicians On Call, which he began supporting in 2011. The organization has over thirty-four participating musicians and has made a difference in countless lives. The group brings volunteer performers to the bedsides of patients all across the world. In addition to making hospital stays more pleasant, the activity is motivated by the musicians' own observations of music's ability to help patients. Research continues to document the health benefits of music in achieving genuine happiness and health.

In serving as a volunteer for this organization, Mars joins in bringing the thrill and joy of a private concert to people who are ill.

Rainforest Foundation

Mars has also expressed some very meaningful concerns by performing to raise money for the Rainforest Foundation, a New York City–based organization he started supporting in 2012. Most people imagine that this organization primarily seeks to raise environmental awareness about rainforests. However, the foundation is actually devoted to protecting the rights of indigenous groups that live within the rainforest.

In addition to the devastation that exploiting rainforests has on the environment and the animals, it also affects the lives of population groups such as the Kayapo, natives who live within the Brazilian Amazon. In using his talents to raise money for this organization, Mars shows his honest concern for marginalized groups and helps to fight for the rights of a population that many of his fans do not even know exists.

International Federation of Red Cross and Red Crescent Societies

Mars is known for being willing to act quickly to assist those who need it the most. This is the case with the Red Cross, which provides relief to disaster areas, whether they are man-made or natural tragedies. For Mars, this included people in the Philippines whose lives were nearly destroyed by 2013's Typhoon Haiyan, which was also known as Super Typhoon Yolanda. Along with other artists—such as Eminem, Imagine Dragons, Pitbull, and Beyoncé—he contributed music for the album SONGS FOR THE PHILLIPINES, which was released globally on November 25, 2013. All proceeds from the album went to assist the victims of Typhoon Haiyan.

He has also worked with the American Red Cross on more domestic issues, including donating tickets to a sold-out Las Vegas show (plus hotel accommodations) to help the Red Cross raise money to educate California residents about earthquake preparedness and to support ongoing earthquake relief efforts in the state.

Whatever Is Needed

Sometimes the charitable contributions Mars makes are financial. For instance, with regard to Super Typhoon Yolanda, he donated $100,000 in 2014 to aid its victims. The storm hit the central Philippines in November 2013, damaging or destroying many cities across the islands and killing over 6,300 residents. The money Mars donated was used for a variety of good causes, including providing immediate medical relief and emergency food supplies to who were sick and starving.

Some of these funds provided long-term assistance—being used to establish special scholarships, provide additional food programs, and teach disaster-preparedness strategies. The donation highlights the commitment Mars has to helping children and adults recover from unthinkable disasters, and helping them rebuild their lives.

Fast Fact 5:

Force of Nature—Super Typhoon Yolanda was particularly devastating, being recorded as one of the most intense tropical cyclones on record. It claimed the lives of over 6,300 people, and over 1,000 people are still missing.

Mama Earth

Perhaps one of the reasons that giving comes so naturally to Mars is that it runs in the family! He frequently assists with the charity Mama Earth, which was created by his sister, Jaime Kailani, in 2009. Much like Mars himself, this particular organization has helped create various artistic events, educational initiatives, and social justice initiatives throughout the entire world. This included providing pop-up sleeping areas for homeless citizens in Los Angeles and holding annual art shows in Santa Monica to showcase the work of creative young adults. With Mars's help, they also raise money for orphanages across the world.

As for Mars, he supports this charity in a number of ways: Sometimes he donates memorabilia, such as signed guitars, to raise funds for orphanages that desperately need money. Other times, he contributes financially to the good causes championed by this charitable organization. He also uses his musical talents in Mama Earth performances, helping them raise money for a variety of causes, such as Nourish the Children.

Overall, Mars's work with Mama Earth clearly demonstrates his dedication to keeping close ties with his family while also making a difference in people's lives—both nationally and internationally.

Flint, Michigan, Water Crisis

Watch an interview with Mars's sister about Mama Earth, where she describes how Mars helps out

One of the best examples of Mars's generosity was his stepping in to assist with a particular crisis that countless politicians have been unable to fix. Like many people, the singer was horrified at the hazardous water problems exposed in Flint, Michigan. The disaster began when the Detroit water system started using water from the Flint River. Unfortunately, it was found that the river was filled with lead, a naturally occurring metal that is harmful to humans, especially to children, even in small doses. It caused a crisis in April of 2014 for Flint residents who were struggling to get access to clean water that had no lead in it.

The crisis was still ongoing in 2017 when Mars donated the revenue from a show in the Detroit area to the Community Foundation of Greater Flint. Ultimately, Mars was able to donate $1 million to this cause, which will go a long way toward helping a city that has been suffering for years.

Worldwide Generosity

Two of Mars's best qualities are his generosity and his desire to directly address the problems affecting people all over the world. As part of this, he contributes to multiple charities that have an emotional impact on the lives of young people. These include Candie's Foundation, which focuses on preventing teenage pregnancy, and DoSomething.Org. This non-profit raises money to help young people who are fighting conditions such as poverty, violence, and environmental issues.

Finally, he contributes to Global Citizen, which focuses on young and old alike by raising money to deal with multiple issues, ranging from child mortality to famine to gender equality. Through his participation with these different organizations, Mars transmits a clear message that he believes in the equality and prosperity of people all across the world.

Overcoming Challenges

It is easy to look at Bruno Mars's success and think he's had a charmed life in which everything came very easily to him. After all, he lives in a **posh** mansion and goes on extravagant world tours where he meets fans in every corner of the planet. However, greatness isn't something a person can achieve without overcoming some very difficult challenges, and even this musical megastar has faced some significant trials in his life. In fact, one of the greatest adversities came from his attempts to become a successful musician!

Beginning Moves

Mars moved to California at the young age of seventeen, fresh out of high school. He decided to move in with his older sister, Jaime, to pursue his music dreams. However, as he recalls, the difference between his vision of life as a music artist and the reality was vast.

"You think it's like the movies, like you get signed and Pharrell and Timbaland are working with you. But it wasn't like that." He realized that instead of relying on a studio to help him make his big start, he needed to "write the song the world is going to want to hear and play over and over again."

The Next Generation—The decision Mars came to—that he had to create everything himself in order to eventually get noticed—is very similar other artists. For instance, many modern YouTubers follow that creative path, using the platform to showcase their artistic talents to the world.

The Right Path to Success

At first, it looked like he had made an early conquest when he signed with the legendary label Universal Motown Records in 2014. However, the demo was terrible. The star later said that he "sounded like a chipmunk," and the label dropped him less than a year later without producing any albums. Mars kept at it, though, and eventually achieved mixed results: Labels liked his songs, but wanted other artists to sing them.

Eventually, Mars recognized that this was his secret path to success.

> *So that's when the light bulb went off. I decided to push the artist thing aside and get into the business this way. We can write songs and produce songs, so we just really focused our energy into writing for other artists. That's how it all began.*

Racism

In the end, of course, Mars achieved success as a singer with his smash hit *Nothin' on You*, followed by a series of amazing singles and subsequent Grammy Award nominations. However, the singer has endured race issues throughout his career. Early on, "record companies were not sure whether to play his songs on pop or urban radio stations" due to his race. Since Mars is "a mixture of Puerto Rican, Jewish, and Filipino heritage," the industry thought it would be difficult to figure out which racial groups to market him to.

Race and Marketing—To maximize profits, record companies try to promote singers and albums to broad groups of people, identified by specific demographics. These statistics often involve race, which is why some in the industry felt that Mars's mixed heritage would make it difficult to find any single demographic sector to promote his music to.

Even his breakout hit, *Nothin' on You*, was subjected to industry racism. In a 2013 interview with *Entertainment Weekly*, Mars recalled a record industry bigwig whose reaction to the song was, "You know what kind of white artist we could break with this? Blond hair, blue eyes, we could make this kid the next thing!" Mars remembered that moment making him feel like a "**mutant**."

Furthermore, he felt like he had to hide his identity to achieve success. His true last name is "Hernandez," but he mentioned in a *GQ* interview of the same year that he kept being encouraged to create Latin music—like Enrique Iglesias—rather than to try to achieve mainstream success. However, his persistence and talent eventually led to the kind of triumph that most singers can only dream about.

Interactions with Other Musicians

Even after overcoming the hurdles of breaking into the music industry and beating its corporate racism, Mars faced another challenge: finding acceptance with rival musicians. One vivid

The Smeezingtons (from left) Philip Lawrence, Bruno Mars and Ari Levine

instance of this occurred in the song *Yonkers*, in which Tyler, The Creator (an American rapper and producer from California who helped form Odd Future Records) graphically sang that he wanted to hurt Mars physically.

Kanye West was less violent but a bit more cutting in his criticism. During one of Kanye's performances in 2013, he complained about how "Bruno Mars won all the ... awards." Kanye went on to imply that Mars had not worked hard enough to deserve these awards, and that he was not well-respected by "the streets." According to Kanye, Mars's success was a result of "networks" and their attempt to "gas everybody up" so they could simply sell a product by using a pretty face.

Isn't It Ironic?—While Kanye West and his criticism of others are both legendary, it is bizarre that he criticized Mars for only being a pretty face without talent that studios were trying to sell. As Mars himself has recounted, some of his earliest struggles as an artist occurred because certain studios wanted to use his musical gifts to launch the careers of others.

Kanye West at the 59th Primetime Emmy Awards at the Shrine Auditorium. September 17, 2007 Los Angeles, CA

Ultimately, each veteran musician ended up eating their words. Tyler, The Creator eventually used his Twitter account to declare that he was wrong about Mars before, and that Mars is "really talented." He admitted that Mars's live performance of *Gorilla* on MTV spotlighted his true talent.

And Kanye went even further in his apology, posting on his Twitter account in February 2015 that he wanted to "publicly apologize," and that Kanye really respects what Mars "does as an artist." He even invited Mars to sing the hook on one of his songs, *88 Keys*. In an unexpected twist, Kanye invited Tyler, The Creator to direct the music video.

This reveals how Mars and his commitment to improving—as an artist, writer, and musician—helped him eventually win over even his biggest haters.

A Personal Loss

A very large hurdle that the singer had to overcome in 2013 was the unexpected death of Mars's mother from a brain **aneurysm**. She was a key influence on her son musically, as a singer and a hula dancer, along with her husband, a percussionist. Collectively, they had given Mars opportunities to explore his musical talents, and they supported him toward his eventual success.

Her sudden death was a major blow to the superstar. However, he overcame the tragedy with quiet grace, posting on Twitter in June 2013 that he was "So thankful for all the love during the most difficult time in my life. I'll be back on my feet again soon. That's what mom wants, she told me."

True to his word, Mars proceeded with his planned world tour (the Moonshine Jungle Tour that ran from June 22, 2013, to October 18, 2014), showing that not even the greatest of family tragedies could slow the singer down.

Text-Dependent Questions:

❶ What medical condition claimed the life of Mars's mother?

❷ With whom did Mars live when he first left Hawaii?

❸ What social media site did both Tyler, The Creator and Kanye West use to apologize to Mars?

Research Project:

Examine your local area and select a charity. Write about how it has made an impact where you live. Next, write about what steps you could take over the next year to work with this charity and begin making a difference in your community.

Series Glossary of Key Terms

A&R: an abbreviation that stands for Artists and Repertoire, which is a record company department responsible for the recruitment and development of talent; similar to a talent scout for sports.

ambient: a musical style that relies on electronic sounds, gentle music, and the lack of a regular beat to create a relaxed mood for the listener.

brand: a particular product or a characteristic that serves to identify a particular product; a brand name is one having a well-known and usually highly regarded or marketable word or phrase.

cameo: also called a cameo role; a minor part played by a prominent performer in a single scene of a motion picture or a television show.

choreography: the art of planning and arranging the movements, steps, and patterns of dancers.

collaboration: a product created by working with someone else; combining individual talents.

debut: a first public appearance on a stage, on television, or so on, or the beginning of a profession or career; the first appearance of something, like a new product.

deejay (DJ): a slang term for a person who spins vinyl records on a turntable; aka a disc jockey.

demo: a recording of a new song, or of one performed by an unknown singer or group, distributed to disc jockeys, recording companies, and the like, to demonstrate the merits of the song or performer.

dubbed: something that is named or given a new name or title; in movies, when the actors' voices have been replaced with those of different performers speaking another language; in music, transfer or copying of previously recorded audio material from one medium to another.

endorsement: money earned from a product recommendation, typically by a celebrity, athlete, or other public figure.

entrepreneur: a person who organizes and manages any enterprise, especially a business, usually with considerable initiative and at financial risk.

falsetto: a man singing in an unnaturally high voice, accomplished by creating a vibration at the very edge of the vocal chords.

genre: a subgroup or category within a classification, typically associated with works of art, such as music or literature.

hone, honing: sharpening or refining a set of skills necessary to achieve success or perform a specific task.

icon: a symbol that represents something, such as a team, a religious person, a location, or an idea.

innovation: the introduction of something new or different; a brand-new feature or upgrade to an existing idea, method, or item.

instrumental: serving as a crucial means, agent, or tool; of, relating to, or done with an instrument or tool.

jingle: a short verse, tune, or slogan used in advertising to make a product easily remembered.

mogul: someone considered to be very important, powerful, and in charge; a term usually associated with heads of businesses in the television, movie studio, or recording industries.

performing arts: skills that require public performance, as acting, singing, or dancing.

philanthropy: goodwill to fellow members of the human race; an active effort to promote human welfare.

public relations: the activity or job of providing information about a particular person or organization to the public so that people will regard that person or organization in a favorable way.

sampler: a digital or electronic musical instrument, related to a synthesizer, that uses samples, or sound recordings, of real instruments (trumpet, violin, piano, etc.) mixed with excerpts of recorded songs and other interesting sounds (sirens, ocean waves, construction noises, car horns, etc.) that are stored digitally and can be replayed by a triggering device, like a sequencer, electronic drums, or a MIDI keyboard.

single: a music recording having two or more tracks that is shorter than an album, EP, or LP; also, a song that is particularly popular, independent of other songs on the same album or by the same artist.

Further Reading

Cohen, Nadia and Alice Hudson. *Bruno Mars: An Unofficial Biography*. London: Flame Tree Publishing, 2013.

Herbert, Emily. *Bruno Mars*. London: Omnibus Press, 2014.

Higgins, Nadia. *Bruno Mars: Pop Singer and Producer*. Minneapolis: Lerner Publishing, 2012.

Nelson, Kristen Rajczak. *Bruno Mars: Singer and Songwriter*. New York: Enslow Publishing, 2016.

Strand, Jennifer. *Bruno Mars*. Minneapolis: ABDO Publishing, 2016.

Internet Resources

www.billboard.com
The official site of Billboard Music.

www.brunomars.com
The official website of Bruno Mars.

4mamaearth.org
The official website of Mama Earth, the charity started by Mars's sister.

https://www.youtube.com/channel/UCoUM-UJ7rirJYP8CQ0EIaHA
The official YouTube channel of Bruno Mars, including many official music videos.

https://www.grammy.com/grammys/artists/bruno-mars
Read information about the Grammy Awards Mars has received, and the latest news about the singer.

Citations

"We've come a long way…" Bruno Mars, as quoted by Zach Seemayer. "Bruno Mars Says Fans Can Expect a Lot More Music in Heartfelt Acceptance Speech: 'I'm Just Getting Started.'" ET Online. March 05, 2017.

"I really feel so strong about it…" Bruno Mars. Interview by Gillian Orr. *The Independent*. December 09, 2012.

"I'm just trying to figure out why…" Bruno Mars. Interview by Josh Eells. *Rolling Stone*. November 02, 2016.

"Moist dishcloth…" Lauren O'Neill. *Vice*. November 11, 2016.

"Suffer." Mars, as quoted by Just Jared. JustJared.com. October 05, 2010.

"Out of frustration." Mars, as quoted by Brad Wete. *Entertainment Weekly*. April 13, 2010.

"Do more…" Mars, as quoted by Georgette Cline. *Rap-Up*. May 11, 2010.

"Two feet tall." Mars, as quoted by John Berger. *Honolulu Star-Advertiser*. April 22, 2014.

"A shadow." Jon Caramanica. *New York Times*. October 05, 2010.

"White artist." Mars, as quoted by Leah Greenblatt. *Entertainment Weekly*. May 17, 2013.

"Obsess…" Mars, as quoted by Hamish McBain. *NME*. November 18, 2016.

"Doo-wop." Mars, as quoted by Bain. Idolator. August 31, 2010.

"It's probably the worst feeling…" Mars, as quoted by NPR. NPR. December 03, 2010.

"Go to hell." Mars, as quoted by CBS. CBS. December 06, 2012.

"You think it's like…" Mars, as quoted by Watson. Stephanie Watson. *Bruno Mars: Pop Superstar* (Minnesota: ABDO Publishing, 2014), 30.

"So that's when…" Mars, as quoted by Moniz. Melissa Moniz. *MidWeek*, April 14, 2010.

"Record companies were…" Watson, 35.

"You know what kind of white artist…" Mars, as quoted by Greenblatt.

"Bruno Mars won all the…" West, as quoted by Willis. Jackie Willis. ET Online. November 21, 2013.

"Really talented." Tyler, The Creator. Twitter post. April 24, 2015.

"Publicly apologize…" Kanye West, as quoted by Maya Rhodan. *Time* (magazine). February 26, 2015.

"So thankful…" Bruno Mars. Twitter post. June 06, 2013.

Educational Videos

Chapter 1:
http://x-qr.net/1GYq
http://x-qr.net/1Czz
http://x-qr.net/1DRL
http://x-qr.net/1H1m
http://x-qr.net/1ECo
http://x-qr.net/1Fc5

Chapter 2:
http://x-qr.net/1Hd7

Chapter 3:
http://x-qr.net/1Gj6

Chapter 4:
http://x-qr.net/1F0y

Chapter 5:
http://x-qr.net/1HjP

Photo Credits

Chapter 1:
Bruno_Mars_keyboard.jpg | Wikimedia Commons
ID 55018392 © Starstock | Dreamstime
ID 52524739 © Jaguarps | Dreamstime
ID 24036846 © Carrienelson1 | Dreamstime
Bruno_Mars_2010.jpg | Wikimedia Commons
Bruno_Mars_Atlanta_concert.jpg | Wikimedia
Commons
Bruno_Mars_Concert.jpg | Wikimedia Commons

Chapter 2:
ID 22767984 © Featureflash | Dreamstime
ID 23476337 © Featureflash | Dreamstime
Bruno_Mars_Concert_2.jpg | Wikimedia Commons
BrunoMars.jpg | Wikimedia Commons
ID 25007025 © Sbukley | Dreamstime
ID 25283922 © Carrienelson1 | Dreamstime
ID 25133265 © Sbukley | Dreamstime
ID 21036802 © Randy Miramontez | Dreamstime
ID 34829449 © Featureflash | Dreamstime
ID 7348253 © Noam Wind | Dreamstime
ID 28660317 © Marsia16 | Dreamstime

Chapter 3:
85217387@N04/8447411547 | Themeplus | Flickr
ID 26355526 © Sbukley | Dreamstime
Bruno_Mars_b%26w.jpg | Wikimedia Commons
8055/8447410717_262cc5e228.jpg | Flickr
Bruno_Mars_Doo-Wops_%26_Hooligans_Black_and_
White.jpg | Wikimedia Commons

Chapter 4:
Bruno_Mars_Concert_Houston_3.jpg | Wikimedia
Commons
Bruno_Mars_in_his_Moonshine_Jungle_Tour_at_
Madison_Square_Garden.jpg | Wikimedia Commons
5206867765 | Brothers Le | Flickr

Chapter 5:
14771153@N04/23499426318 | slgckgc | Flickr
ID 25007025 © Sbukley | Dreamstime
ID 89718608 © Esmehelit | Dreamstime
ID 26273881 © Americanspirit | Dreamstime
Bruno_Mars_Super_Bowl.jpg | Arnie Papp | Wikimedia
Commons
ID 23475044 © Sbukley | Dreamstime
ID 24605019 © Featureflash | Dreamstime

Index

Index

Index

Author's Biography

Chris Snellgrove received a PhD in English from Auburn University in 2012. In addition to publishing several academic texts and educational materials, he is a veteran online writer for websites such as Listverse, Grunge, Looper, and Screenrant. His academic specialty was American literature, but his later interest (in terms of both academic and freelance writing) has been pop culture. He has spoken at academic conferences throughout America and currently serves as an assistant professor of English at Northwest Florida State College in Niceville, Florida, and he lives in Crestview, Florida, with his wife, son, and two dogs.